Freezer Meals: Delicious and Easy Make-Ahead Meals

by Rashelle Johnson

© 2012, Michael Anderson. All rights reserved.

This book contains material protected under International and Federal Copyright Laws and Treaties. Any unauthorized reprint or use of this material is prohibited. No part of this book may be reproduced or transmitted in any form or by any means, electronic or mechanical, including photocopying, recording, or by any information storage and retrieval system without express written permission from the author.

Disclaimer:

The information contained in this book is for general information purposes only. This book is sold with the understanding the author and/or publisher is not giving medical advice, nor should this book replace medical advice, nor is it intended to diagnose or treat any disease, illness or other medical condition.

While we endeavor to keep the information up to date and correct, we make no representations or warranties of any kind, express or implied, about the completeness, accuracy, reliability, suitability or availability with respect to the book or the information, products, services, or related graphics contained book for any purpose. Any reliance you place on such information is therefore strictly at your own risk.

In no event will we be liable for any liability, loss or damage including without limitation, indirect or consequential loss or damage, or any loss or damage whatsoever arising from loss of data or profits arising out of, or in connection with, the use of the material or the interpretation of the material contained in this book.

Dedication:

This is dedicated to my friends and family members who had to endure recipe after recipe while I was writing this book. Thanks for all your help. I love you guys and promise not to force you to try anything new … At least until I write my next cookbook.

Contents

What Are Freezer Meals? 7
Planning a Cooking Session 8
Storing Freezer Meals 12
Individual Quick Freezing Prevents Foods from Sticking Together 15
Think of the Freezer as a Pause Button 16
Foods that Can Be Frozen 18
    Breads and Rolls 18
    Brownies 19
    Butter and Margarine 19
    Cheese 19
    Cookies 20
    Cake and Cupcakes 20
    Candy 21
    Casseroles and Enchiladas 21
    Chocolate and Fudge 21
    Eggs 22
    Fruit 22
    Herbs and Spices 23
    Homemade Granola 23
    Jam and Jelly 23
    Lasagna 23

100% Maple Syrup 24

Meat and Fish 24

Milk 24

Muffins and Biscuits 25

Nuts and Seeds 25

Soups and Chilies 26

Pasta 26

Pies 27

Rice and Brown Rice 27

Vegetables 27

Wine 27

Foods You Shouldn't Freeze 29

How to Safely Thaw Your Food 31

Freezer Meal Recipes 33

Freezer Chicken Enchiladas 34

Tasty Turkey Taco Soup 37

Frozen Minestrone Soup 39

Crock Pot Ham and Pineapple 41

Bacon-Wrapped Chicken Breasts 42

Cheesy Buttermilk Biscuits 44

Buttermilk Pancakes 46

Frozen Shrimp Egg Rolls 48

Make-Ahead Pork Fried Rice 52

Freezer Lasagna 54

Honey Dijon Salmon 57

Shredded Slow-Cooked Beef Sandwiches 59

Spaghetti and Meatball Casserole 61

Freezer Cheesy Garlic Bread 63

Mini Meatloaf Bites 64

Baked Whole Wheat Penne Casserole with Sausage 66

Grilled Chicken Skewers 68

Other Titles by This Author 70

What Are Freezer Meals?

If you've ever had a TV dinner, you've had a freezer meal. Well, sort of.

The processed food in a TV dinner can hardly be called a meal. It doesn't taste very good and we eat it purely out of convenience when we don't have the time, energy or willpower to cook.

What most people don't realize is there are much better options out there than TV dinners and fast food when you're looking for a quick and easy meal.

Instead of buying frozen pre-cooked foods at the store, you can cook a wide variety of foods at home ahead of time and freeze them so they'll be ready to make when you need something quick and easy. The best part about making homemade freezer meals is you get to choose what goes in them. You can make them delicious and healthy, and you can forgo all the nitrates and additives that are added to most commercially-sold frozen foods.

You get the best of both worlds and only have to do a little bit of extra work.

There are a couple ways to go about making freezer meals. The first, and easiest, way to build up a collection of freezer meals is to triple or quadruple your recipes when you cook dinner and then freeze the leftovers. This will give you 2 to 3 extra meals every time you cook. On the days you don't feel like cooking, you can whip out a freezer meal and be done with dinner in no time flat.

The other way to cook freezer meals is to designate a day or two each month and spend a good portion of the day cooking.

If the idea of a whole day in the kitchen terrifies you, it's time to call in the cavalry. Throw a freezer meal party, in which each person cooks enough of one recipe to give a serving to everyone else in the party. You only have to cook one recipe and end up with a variety of meals you can freeze and serve later.

Having a stock of freezer meals can be a lifesaver for those days when life gets in the way of cooking dinner. You just pull something out, thaw it and warm it up.

Don't limit yourself to just dinner when it comes to freezer meals. A number of snacks, desserts and lunch and breakfast items can be prepared ahead of time and frozen, too.

You can cook as many as 50 meals or more in a single day if you're willing to work. Cooking dinner will be a breeze and you can make enough different meals so that your family won't complain about having the same thing every night. You could make enough food in a day or two to take *months* off from cooking meals. That is, if you have a big enough freezer.

Planning a Cooking Session

If you decide to whip up a bunch of freezer meals in a single session, you're going to want to plan your course of attack ahead of time. Planning allows you to maximize the time spent in the kitchen.

The first item on the agenda is planning what you're going to cook. Try not to overdo it the first few times you cook freezer meals. You're going to be cooking batches of food that are a lot bigger than what you're used to cooking and you're going to have to pay close attention to what you're doing. I'd suggest only making 1 or 2 foods the first time you make freezer meals. If everything goes well with a couple meals, then you can expand out and make more meals the next time.

The most important part of planning is making sure you have everything you need ahead of time. Nothing stalls out a day of cooking freezer meals like having to take multiple unanticipated trips to the store to purchase ingredients. I like to plan out my cooking days a month or two in advance, so I can watch for coupons and sales on the ingredients I'm going to need for my recipes.

Take each of the recipes you plan on cooking and multiply each of the ingredient quantities by the number of extra meals you want to make. For example, if you have a recipe that normally makes 1 meal and you want to make 4 freezer meals, multiply the amount of each of the ingredients by 4. A recipe that requires 1 cup of milk will now require 4 cups of milk in the new recipe. Write the new quantities out on the old recipe or make a new recipe with the new quantities and print it out.

Once you've figured out the ingredients you're going to need, you need to make a shopping list. If you're anything like me, you'll want to write down the items you need, or you run the risk of getting home and realizing you forgot something important. Go shopping a couple days in advance and make sure you have everything on hand on cooking day.

Here's a tip that might help prevent you from making a rookie mistake that I made my first big cooking day. Don't forget the containers. Make sure you have enough freezer bags and containers on hand to store the meals you're making. I finished cooking a big batch of soup one evening only to find I didn't have any sealable bowls or freezer bags left. I had to take a trip to Wal-Mart at 11PM at night. You don't ever want to go to Wal-Mart at that time of night. Trust me on this one.

You also want to clear out room in your freezer. Make sure you have room ahead of time by cooking some of the foods you've had in there for a while and eating them in the days leading up to cooking day—or you can just throw out that huge hunk of venison your uncle gave you 4 years ago. He'll never know, I promise.

If you plan on making freezer meals a big part of your life, a standalone freezer isn't a bad idea. You'll have a lot more room to store meals and you'll have the freezer in your refrigerator free for other stuff.

The next step is to pick a day and let everyone know you aren't to be disturbed. If you have older kids and a spouse, you can enlist their help if you so desire. My kids and husband hinder my efforts more than they help, so I do all the cooking and turn the cleaning of the kitchen over to them. Turnaround is fair play—and I enjoy cooking a lot more than I enjoy cleaning. I knew having those darn kids would pay off someday.

Plan ahead of time what order you're going to cook your food in. I like to have a pot or two going on the stove and at least one item cooking in the oven. My record so far is 4 meals going at once. I cooked two soups, a lasagna and slow-cooked beef all at the same time during my last cooking day. I also managed to partially cook my pinky finger, but that's a completely different story.

When cooking day comes, wake up and eat breakfast, then get to work. Put your nose to the grindstone and knock out as many meals as you can fit in your freezer. Package each meal as you finish cooking it and move on to the next one.

Clean up and pat yourself on the back. It's going to be a while before you have to cook again!

Storing Freezer Meals

When you plan out your freezer meals, it's important to plan out how and where you're going to store them. You don't want to come up short on storage containers or find you have to throw away perfectly good food to make room in the freezer for your meals.

You can use whatever you'd like to store your foods in the freezer. For long-term storage, you want to use sealable plastic bags or airtight storage containers like Tupperware.

For short-term storage, you can even get away with wrapping the food in aluminum foil and freezing it. I wouldn't recommend storing foods this way for more than a few days because you'll end up with something that looks like it was dipped in liquid nitrogen. Freezer burn can ruin foods that aren't properly packaged in less than a week. There's nothing worse than going to grab a quick meal from the freezer only to find all of your meals are ruined. Not only has the hard work it took you to make the meals gone to waste, you'll have to make dinner from scratch. Who has time for that?

The majority of my meals are stored in freezer bags. They work great for sauces, soups, chilies, meats and any number of other foods that can be fit in the bags, which not coincidentally come in a range of sizes that can fit anything from a few ants to an aircraft carrier.

I prefer the Ziploc bags because they have the white stripe on the front on which I can neatly print what's in the bag and the date the bag was put in the freezer. Label everything. You might think you'll remember what's in the bag, but after you cook a few freezer meals and stuff migrates to the back of the freezer, you aren't going to know what's in the bag after it's been frozen a while.

In order to get liquid soups and runny dishes into a freezer baggie, place the baggie in a Mason jar or can and fold the top of the bag over the edges. This will allow you to pour hot liquid into the bag without having to worry about keeping the bag under control. Remember earlier when I said I partially cooked my pinky? I did it trying to hold a baggie open without placing it in a jar for support. Trust me, hot soup can do a number on your finger. I'm just glad the spill didn't hit the rest of my hand!

Tupperware and Pyrex containers come in handy also, but they tend to take up more room than the freezer bags. When I first started making freezer meals, I used Pyrex containers more than Ziploc bags, but lately I've been using Ziplocs for almost everything. It allows me to store more food and saves me the hassle of having to put a piece of masking tape on the Pyrex containers to label them. There's a lot less wasted air space in a Ziploc baggie than there is in a plastic container, which means more space in the freezer—which means less time spent cooking for me!

Casseroles and lasagna dishes can be cooked and stored in the glass dish you cooked them in. Thrift stores and flea markets are great places to find extra glass dishes. If you don't want to store glass dishes, line your casserole dish with aluminum foil before baking the casserole. Place the dish in the freezer until the casserole is partially frozen to make it more manageable. Lift the foil out of the dish and divide the casserole into single meal-sized sections and wrap each section in foil. Place the foil-covered casserole meals in individual freezer baggies and seal them up airtight for storage.

Here's a tip that'll help you save on your electrical bill. If your freezer is empty, it's going to have to work harder to keep the open air in the freezer cold. A full freezer is much more efficient when it comes to electricity usage than an empty freezer. If you find your freezer is emptying out, you can save energy by filling a few gallon jugs with water and putting them in the freezer to fill the space.

One last tip on storage—and this one's a big one. Whenever possible, cool your food in the fridge before freezing it. Food that's cooked and then put in the freezer warm is more prone to freezer burn than food that's cooled and then frozen.

You're going to want to track what you have in the freezer, so there's no guesswork when dinner time rolls around. I have a magnetic clipboard stuck to the side of my freezer that has all of the meals in it listed on a sheet of paper. Every time I pull something out or put something in, it gets added to or removed from the list.

Individual Quick Freezing Prevents Foods from Sticking Together

This chapter is going to be short, but the information here is important.

Anyone with any experience with freezer meals will tell you that certain types of foods like berries, muffins, cookies and meat patties tend to stick together during the freezing process. It doesn't affect the taste or nutritional value, but it can be a hassle getting them apart without destroying them.

You can combat this tendency of certain foods to stick together by individual quick freezing (IQF) the foods before storing them.

IQF sounds a lot harder than it actually is.

All you need to do to IQF food is to freeze the items individually until they start to firm up. Once firm, you can throw them in a bag and they won't stick together. Spread the items out on a tray or a pan so they aren't touching and put them in the freezer. Come back in a half hour or so and they'll be ready to be thrown in bags—and you'll have saved yourself a lot of hassle later on down the road.

Think of the Freezer as a Pause Button

People tend to think of the freezer as the end of the road for their foods. They get stuck in the mindset that everything in a freezer meal has to be fully cooked before it goes in the freezer.

That really isn't the case. You can use the freezer to pause most meals anywhere in the cooking process. While you wouldn't want to do something odd like cook bread halfway and then freeze it, you could make the dough and then freeze it and cook it later. Baked items sometimes taste better if the dough or batter is frozen, and you thaw it and cook it when you want to eat it.

Some items are better off left uncooked when they're frozen. It's up to you to experiment and figure out the best ways to store the foods you're cooking. Avoid getting stuck on thinking you have to cook everything before throwing it in the freezer.

One item that instantly comes to mind when I think of foods that are better off left uncooked when frozen is lasagna. You can make lasagna and put it in the freezer uncooked. Pull it out and throw the frozen lasagna in the oven. It'll take longer to bake, but it'll taste almost exactly like you made the lasagna right there on the spot.

Another item that does better off when paused partway through the process is soup that has milk-based sauce. Prepare the soup and the sauce separately and freeze it in separate bags, then combine and cook when you want to eat them.

Foods that Can Be Frozen

The title of this chapter is somewhat of a misnomer. It should be titled "Foods that Do Well When Frozen." Most foods can be frozen. You just might not want to eat them once they thaw out.

The good news is there are a lot of foods you can freeze. Foods you wouldn't expect to do well in the freezer like cupcakes and cookies can be frozen and thawed out later. Always let your foods cool before tossing them in the freezer. It helps prevent freezer burn.

The amount of time you can store foods is based on a number of variables and the recommendations for the foods listed in this chapter aren't set in stone. Foods stored in the freezer won't ever really go bad as long as the temperature is 0°F or below. What happens is the quality of the food suffers and it won't taste the way you expect it to and it won't have the same texture.

The following foods can be frozen for consumption at a later time:

Breads and Rolls

For short-term storage, you can wrap your breads and rolls in aluminum foil or plastic wrap and throw them in the freezer. If you want to store them for longer than a week or two, double bag them in plastic freezer bags.

Thaw your bread and rolls out by placing them in the refrigerator and letting them sit overnight. Properly wrapped bread will last up to 6 months in the freezer.

Brownies

That's right, brownies can be frozen. Put them in freezer bags or in airtight containers and you can store them in the freezer for up to 6 months. When you want to eat them, pull them out and let them thaw to room temperature.

Butter and Margarine

If you get a good deal on butter or margarine, you can stock up and put the extra in the freezer. The fresher the butter is when you buy it; the longer it'll last in the freezer. You can freeze fresh butter for 6 to 8 months before the taste and texture start to change.

For best results, freeze butter and margarine in its original container. If the container isn't airtight, put it in a freezer bag before freezing it.

Cheese

I used to have a lot of trouble when I tried to freeze cheese. I'd throw a block of it in the freezer and pull it out when I needed it. Then it would crumble into little chunks that were difficult to do anything with. I gave up trying to freeze blocks of cheese until I went to a friend's house and watched as she pulled a bag of mozzarella out of the freezer *already grated*. It was one of those smack your head moments.

Slice or grate your cheese before you freeze it and it will be more manageable when you defrost it. Defrost frozen cheeses by placing them in the fridge and letting them thaw out. Frozen cheese will last for up to 6 months in the freezer.

While your average everyday cheeses can be frozen and thawed out and eaten with little change to the taste and structure, you want to avoid freezing fine cheeses. The ice crystals that form in cheese when it's frozen can destroy a fine cheese. You're better off storing fine cheeses in the fridge and eating them before they go bad. A good rule of thumb is that it's OK to freeze cheese that you plan on using for cooking, but not cheese you plan on eating plain.

Cookies

Cookies are another item you normally wouldn't think of freezing. Individual quick freezing works well to keep the dough balls from sticking together.

While you can bake your cookies and store them, I prefer making the dough, dividing it into balls and storing the dough. When I want to make a batch of cookies, I pull a bag out and remove as many cookies as I want to make.

You can let them thaw to room temperature before baking, or you can throw them in the over frozen and bake them that way, but it's going to take 5 to 10 minutes longer to cook them.

Cookie dough will keep for 6 months to a year in the freezer depending on the type of dough.

Cake and Cupcakes

You can freeze cupcakes and cakes after baking them. I've heard of people frosting them and freezing them with the frosting on, but I prefer to frost them after thawing them out. Certain types of frosting don't do well in the freezer and frosting is easy enough to make that I don't mind making it on the spot.

Cakes and cupcakes can be double bagged in freezer bags or they can be sealed in airtight plastic containers. They'll last 3 to 6 months in the freezer before they start to degrade.

Candy

Find a good deal after the holidays and stock up. Frozen candy will last until the next time the holiday comes around and you won't have to pay a premium for it the next time around. That is, as long as your kids don't find your stash and munch it down before the holiday comes back around.

Casseroles and Enchiladas

When you make dinner, make extra casseroles and enchiladas and freeze them. You can even make an entire casserole and freeze it in the glass dish you cooked it in. Just make sure you let it cool before tossing it in the freezer. You don't want to be picking glass slivers out of your freezer if the difference in temperatures causes the glass dish to break.

Casseroles and enchiladas should be consumed within 3 months of freezing them.

Chocolate and Fudge

Wrap chocolate and fudge in plastic wrap and store it in a plastic freezer bag. Fudge stays fresh for up to 3 months and chocolate lasts even longer. Avoid freezing lighter fudge and fudge that contains imitation vanilla, as they tend to lose flavor and the texture changes when they're frozen.

Place chocolate and fudge in the fridge to defrost it. Once the frost is gone, move it to room temperature and unwrap it, then let it finish thawing.

Eggs

Here's a strange one most people don't know about. You can freeze egg in the freezer. You don't want to just toss a carton of eggs in because you'll end up with a mess on your hands when the shells crack as they expand. Instead, crack your egg into a bowl, whisk it until the yolk and the white are combined and pour the mixture into an ice tray. Once the egg cubes are frozen, take them out of the tray and store them in freezer bags.

Eggs will last up to 6 months in the freezer.

Fruit

Fruit you plan on using in smoothies or for cooking can be frozen for 3 to 6 months. Individual Quick Freezing works well to keep sticky fruits from sticking to one another as they freeze. Store fruit in plastic freezer bags and double bag it to make sure smells and tastes aren't transferred to other foods.

I don't recommend storing fruit you plan on eating raw in the freezer. When fruit thaws out, it tends to get a bit soggy and won't taste or feel exactly the same as it does when fresh.

Herbs and Spices

If you grow your own herbs and spices, you can freeze them in an ice cube tray. Pack them tightly into the tray and add a bit of water to the top. Freeze them into cubes, then transfer them into freezer bags for safe keeping. When you want to use the frozen herbs or spices, simply pull out a cube and toss it into whatever dish it is you may be cooking. Fresh herbs and spices last up to 6 months stored in the freezer.

Homemade Granola

When I first heard of freezing homemade granola I was surprised. It has a pretty good shelf life and can last a few months out of the freezer. When I incredulously asked the person why they'd freeze granola, they told me it lasts for up to a year in the freezer.

Use a freezer bag or store it in an airtight container.

Jam and Jelly

Instead of canning your jams and jellies, you can freeze them instead. Just be aware that an extended power outage can wipe out a lot of hard work in one fell swoop. Frozen jam will last up to a year in the freezer before it starts degrading.

Lasagna

Prepare the lasagna like you normally would, but instead of popping it in the oven, put it in the freezer. Cooked lasagna can be frozen as well, but it tastes much better if you freeze it uncooked and cook it on the day you wish to eat it. Frozen lasagna will last 4 to 6 months.

100% Maple Syrup

If you find a rare great deal on pure maple syrup, you can freeze it and store it for a year or two before it has to be used. Thaw it out by setting it on the counter and it'll go back to being like new. If sugar crystals form in the syrup, warm it in a saucepan until the crystals melt away.

Meat and Fish

Meat is one of the most common items that people store in the freezer. Bag it or double bag it in freezer bags and you can store meat for as long as a year before it has to be consumed.

Fish can also be stored in the freezer. I recommend wrapping it in plastic wrap, then double bagging it because the aroma and even some of the flavor of fish can be imparted to nearby foods if you aren't careful.

Milk

Milk can be frozen, but you might not enjoy drinking it as much after you thaw it out. The fat separates away from the liquid a bit during the freezing process and it can slightly change the way milk tastes and feels in your mouth as you drink it. It won't hurt you, but it's not exactly the same as drinking a cup of fresh milk. You can mitigate this effect a bit by shaking the carton before drinking it, but it still won't completely eliminate the difference. I don't really like the difference in taste and texture, so I only freeze milk I plan on using for cooking.

If you're going to freeze your milk don't wait until it reaches the "use before" date. Buy the freshest milk you can find and freeze it as soon as you get home. Frozen milk can be stored in the freezer for 3 to 4 months.

Thaw your milk out by putting it in the fridge for a day or two or setting it in a sink full of *cold* water. Don't put it in warm water and don't leave it sitting on the counter to thaw.

Muffins and Biscuits

Already-baked muffins and biscuits can be placed in a large freezer bag and stored for 3 to 6 months in the freezer.

You can also pour the batter into a muffin pan and freeze individual servings of batter. Fill the cups and place the entire tin in the freezer. Once the batter is frozen, pop it out of the tin, bag it up and save it. When you want to bake muffins, put each serving back into the muffin pan and let it thaw out before baking.

Nuts and Seeds

I didn't even know nuts and seeds could go bad until I read about it in one of my cookbooks. Apparently the oil in them can go rancid if you store your nuts at room temperature. While I've never had this happen, I guess it isn't beyond the realm of possibility.

Pack nuts and seeds in freezer bags before storing them in the freezer. You're going to want to double bag them because nuts can pick up scents and flavors from other foods stored in the same general area.

I couldn't find any reliable information on how long nuts and seeds could be stored in the freezer. Some sources say they'll last up to 6 months, but mine last at least that long in the pantry. You could probably store your nuts and seeds in the freezer for a year or longer.

Soups and Chilies

You can freeze most soups and chilies and store them for up to a year in the freezer. They can be frozen in airtight containers or freezer bags. I prefer freezer bags because I can fit more of them into my freezer.

You may occasionally come across a soup that doesn't do well when frozen. Soups with milk-based sauces don't freeze very well when the sauce is mixed with the rest of the ingredients. Boil the ingredients separately from the sauce and freeze the sauce and the rest of the soup in two separate bags. Combine the contents of each bag and warm it up when you're ready to eat it.

Pasta

Cook your pasta, but don't add the sauce to it. Add a bit of olive oil instead and toss it until it's lightly coated. Bag it in single-serving portions and freeze it. Cook and bag the sauces separately. When it comes time to serve the pasta for dinner, combine the pasta and the sauce and heat them up. You can heat frozen pasta in the microwave for a quick and easy meal.

Pasta and sauce will last up to 6 months in the freezer.

Pies

You can freeze entire pies before they're baked. Some pies can be frozen after baking them, but I've found it leaves them a little soggy. Wrap the pie plate snugly in plastic wrap. Use a few layers for best results.

Pies will last for up to 6 months when frozen.

Rice and Brown Rice

If you eat a lot of rice, make a large batch and freeze it. You can freeze it in freezer bags or airtight plastic containers. White rice will last for 3 to 6 months in the freezer. Brown rice doesn't last as long and should be used before you reach the 3-month mark.

Vegetables

Most vegetables can be frozen and thawed with little to no change to the taste or texture. Blanch your vegetables by submerging them in boiling water for a few minutes and then place them directly into cool water and let them chill for the same amount of time before you freeze them.

You can bag vegetables in freezer bags or you can store them in sealable containers. Properly blanched and cooled vegetables can last as long as 12 to 18 months in the freezer.

Wine

How often do you find yourself pouring wine down the drain because you didn't finish the bottle before it went bad? If this is a common occurrence, you can save your wine by freezing it in an ice cube tray. You won't want to drink it once it's been frozen, but it works great in recipes that call for wine.

You can store frozen wine for up to a year in the freezer if you transfer the frozen cubes from the ice tray to a freezer bag.

Foods You Shouldn't Freeze

While you may be tempted to freeze everything in your path, especially when you're first getting started, there are some foods that don't survive freezing and subsequent defrosting very well.

When you freeze and defrost the following foods, the quality almost always suffers:

- **Canned foods.**
- **Celery.**
- **Cloves.**
- **Cooked eggs.**
- **Cottage cheese.**
- **Cream cheese.**
- **Cream.**
- **Cucumbers.**
- **Custard.**
- **Eggs in the shell.**
- **Fried foods.**
- **Garlic.**
- **Imitation vanilla.**
- **Leafy greens like lettuce and cabbage.**
- **Many raw fruits and veggies.**
- **Mayonnaise.**
- **Onions.**
- **Pepper.**
- **Peppers.**
- **Plain yogurt.**
- **Potatoes.**

- **Sage.**
- **Sauces that contain wheat.**
- **Skim milk.**
- **Soft cheeses.**
- **Sour cream.**
- **Store-bought frosting.**
- **Tomatoes.**
- **Watermelon.**
- **Whole avocados.**

I want you to be aware that this isn't an exhaustive list. This is just a list of things I know don't make it through the freezing and thawing process intact. If you aren't sure about something, try freezing and thawing a small portion. That way, you don't ruin an entire meal (or meals) by freezing something that doesn't do well in the freezer.

How to Safely Thaw Your Food

There are 4 ways you can safely thaw your food out when you wish to eat it. Thawing your food out in any way other than the following 4 ways can make your food unsafe to eat.

Never let food sit out on the counter or set it in the sun to thaw. You don't want to put food outside to thaw because you open it up to all sorts of contamination. Keep it inside and stick to these 4 methods and you should be fine.

Here are the only ways you should thaw your food:

- **Thaw it in the microwave.** Most microwaves have a defrost setting you can use to thaw your food. Be careful thawing out meats with the microwave because it can partially cook the meat while it's defrosting it.
- **In the fridge.** Take the food you want to eat out the night before and put it in the fridge. It should thaw out overnight. Large items like hams and turkeys may need a couple days in the fridge before they thaw out.
- **In cold water.** Make sure your food is stored in a waterproof plastic bag before using this method of defrosting. Fill your sink up with cold water and place the item in the water. This method works faster than the previous two methods. Change the water every half hour until it's thawed.
- **Cook it frozen.** Pop the frozen food in the oven, the microwave or heat it on the stove. Many foods can

be heated up from a frozen state and cooked to perfection. When cooking a frozen food, it usually takes one and a half times the normal time it takes to cook.

Freezer Meal Recipes

While you could probably get away with freezing most of your favorite meals and serving them later, the following recipes are tried and true freezer meals. They've withstood the rigors of freezing and thawing and make it through the ordeal relatively unscathed.

Freezer Chicken Enchiladas

Chicken enchiladas are a favorite dinner in my house. I honestly believe my family would eat them every night if I agreed to serve them that often. These enchiladas are easy to make and taste great after being thawed. If you've never made a freezer meal, this is a great place to start, as it's hard to mess up chicken enchiladas.

This recipe will create 16 enchiladas. You can split them up into meal-sized packages. For my family of four, this creates roughly 3 meals.

Ingredients:

6 cups of tomato sauce

5 cups of boiled chicken, shredded

4 garlic cloves, minced

1 can chipotle chilies

2 tablespoons pickled jalapeno peppers

½ cup cilantro leaves, finely chopped

1 cup chicken broth

2 teaspoons olive oil

2 teaspoons ground cumin

1 ½ teaspoons coriander

1 teaspoon sea salt

16 corn tortillas

Cooking and Freezing Directions:

1. Make enchilada sauce by adding tomato sauce, ground cumin, garlic, onion, chipotle, broth and salt to a blender and pulsing it until smooth.
2. Add the olive oil to a large skillet, pour in the enchilada sauce and bring to a boil. Reduce the heat and let it simmer for 10 minutes. Remove from heat and let cool.
3. Take 2 cups enchilada sauce and the chicken and add it to a large mixing bowl. Stir until the sauce is evenly distributed across the chicken.
4. Add the jalapenos, Monterey jack cheese and the cilantro and mix until it's evenly coated.
5. Spray tortillas with cooking spray and lightly cook them in a frying pan until they start to thicken up. Remove from the pan and fill with the chicken/sauce mixture.
6. Roll the enchilada and place it face down on a plate. You can usually fit 3 to 4 enchiladas on a single plate. Transfer the plate to the freezer. Continue until you're out of chicken.
7. Let the enchiladas freeze on the plates for 45 minutes, then remove them from the freezer and place them in freezer bags. Use one bag per meal.
8. Place the remaining enchilada sauce in separate bag and freeze it.

Defrosting and Reheating Directions:

1. Defrost enchiladas and sauce in the microwave or in the fridge overnight.
2. Spray a baking dish with cooking spray and add a single layer of enchiladas to the dish.

3. Bake for 20 to 25 minutes.
4. Remove from the over and pour the remaining sauce over the enchiladas and sprinkle Mexican blend cheese on top.
5. Bake for another 12 minutes, or until cheese on top is melted.

Tasty Turkey Taco Soup

Taco soup is one of those comfort foods I just can't do without. Whenever I want a quick and tasty meal, this is the one I turn to, especially during the cold winter months when I'm looking for something to warm me up after a long day out in the cold.

This soup can be made quickly the first time you make it and it's even faster to warm up when you pull it out of the freezer.

Ingredients for cooking:

3 pounds ground turkey

2 packs of your favorite taco seasoning

2 16oz cans of corn

2 medium onions, finely chopped

3 16oz cans of black beans

1 28oz cans of crushed tomatoes

1 14oz can of tomato sauce

1 tomato, diced

1 small can diced green chilies

Directions for cooking and freezing:

1. Add the meat to a skillet and cook until it starts to brown. Break it up into medium-sized chunks.
2. Add onions to the pan and cook until they start to turn translucent.
3. Add all of the ingredients to a large cooking pot and stir until they're mixed thoroughly.

4. Let simmer for 40 to 50 minutes or until the tomatoes are cooked. Stir often.
5. Take pot off heat and place in refrigerator until the soup is cool.
6. Bag it in freezer bags or plastic containers and put in freezer.

Ingredients for Reheating:

Sliced avocado

Sour cream

Mexican blend cheese

Tortilla chips

Defrosting and Reheating Directions:

1. Remove soup from freezer and reheat in microwave. Heat it for 2 minutes at a time. Watch closely for it to thaw out and start to warm up. Alternatively, let thaw in the fridge overnight and reheat on the stove.
2. Serve soup hot. Top with sour cream, avocado and cheese. Scoop it out and eat it with tortilla chips or break the tortilla chips up and sprinkle them on top.

Frozen Minestrone Soup

Minestrone soup is a delicious soup that can be served with dinner or as dinner, depending on how industrious you're feeling. Use low-fat stock to make it healthy.

Ingredients:

9 cups chicken stock (use defatted stock if you want it to be healthier)

1 cup sliced green beans

2 16oz cans of kidney beans

1 onion, diced

3 carrots, peeled and diced

1 cup mushrooms, sliced

3 celery sticks, diced

2 14oz cans of stewed tomatoes

2 cloves of garlic, minced

1 cup pasta shells

2 teaspoons dried oregano

2 teaspoons dried basil

1 15oz can of garbanzo beans

2 teaspoons of olive oil

Directions for Preparing and Freezing:

1. Sauté the onions, celery, carrots, green beans and mushrooms in olive oil until lightly browned.
2. Add garlic and sauté for another minute.

3. Combine all ingredients in a large pot and bring to a boil.
4. Let boil for ten minutes. Remove from heat.
5. Let cool for 1 hour in fridge.
6. Transfer to airtight plastic containers or freezer bags and freeze.

Reheating Ingredients:

Parmesan cheese

½ cup chicken stock

Defrosting and Reheating Directions:

1. Transfer frozen soup and ½ cup chicken stock to a large pot and place over low heat.
2. Stir as the soup begins to melt, so the bottom doesn't burn.
3. Bring to a boil. Reduce heat and let simmer for 10 minutes.
4. Remove from heat and let cool for 5 minutes.
5. Serve with parmesan cheese sprinkled on top.

Crock Pot Ham and Pineapple

This recipe is so easy I almost feel guilty including it. To be completely honest with you, it isn't a recipe so much as it is a way to prepare your ham beforehand so it's in family-size servings and ready to toss in the Crockpot.

Ingredients:

Ham

4 cans of pineapple chunks

1 cup brown sugar

Directions for Preparing and Freezing:

7. Add the pineapple chunks (and juice) and brown sugar to a mixing bowl and stir in the brown sugar until it dissolves.
8. Slice the ham and separate it into portions big enough for one meal.
9. Put each meal in a freezer bag and add a liberal amount of pineapple chunks and juice to the bag.
10. Freeze the bag.

Defrosting and Reheating Directions:

1. Move ham from the freezer to the fridge the night before you plan on cooking it. Alternatively, thaw it by setting it in cold water.
2. Set crock pot on high and cook for 3 to 4 hours.

Bacon-Wrapped Chicken Breasts

This is another family favorite. My husband absolutely loves these chicken breasts. They aren't exactly the healthiest choice because of the bacon, but they're sinfully delicious. And the bacon isn't fried, so you do have that.

Like most meats, chicken is best prepared and then frozen prior to cooking it. Freezing it after you cook it will dry it out and change the texture when you warm it back up.

Ingredients:

12 chicken breasts (or however many you feel like wrapping and cooking)

12 slices of bacon

1 clove of garlic, minced

1 tablespoon of rosemary

2 tablespoons olive oil

Directions for Preparing and Freezing:

1. Rub chicken breasts with oil.
2. Rub with liberal amounts of minced garlic and rosemary.
3. Wrap a slice of bacon around each breast.
4. Separate into individual meals and place in freezer bags.
5. Freeze.

Defrosting and Reheating Directions:

1. Preheat oven to 350°F.
2. Cook for 45 to 50 minutes or until done.

3. Serve hot.

Cheesy Buttermilk Biscuits

These cheesy buttermilk biscuits go great with either breakfast or dinner. They don't work well for biscuits and gravy, but they make for a good standalone side for most meals. If you want to switch things up a bit, try adding half a cup of bacon bits to the batter.

Ingredients:

4 eggs

2 ½ tablespoons baking powder

4 cups flour

2 teaspoons salt

1 ½ cups butter

1 cup buttermilk

1 ½ cups shredded cheddar cheese

4 teaspoons milk

Directions for Preparing and Freezing:

1. Add butter, flour, salt and baking powder to a mixing bowl and mix until incorporated. The mixture will be crumbly and should be broken up into chunks the size of your pinky nail when you're done.
2. Add the buttermilk and 2 eggs to the mixture and mix until the batter is moist. Be careful not to mix it too much.
3. Fold the cheese into the dough.

4. Roll out the dough and use a cookie cutter or the top of a glass to cut out muffins. This recipe should make approximately 24 muffins.
5. Add the remaining eggs and the 2 teaspoons of milk to a mixing bowl and whisk together.
6. Lightly coat a baking pan with cooking spray and place the muffins on the pan. Leave an inch or two space between each muffin.
7. Preheat oven to 400°F.
8. Brush the egg/milk mixture onto the top of each muffin.
9. Cook for 15 to 17 minutes or until the muffins start to brown.
10. Place in freezer bags and put them in the freezer. Alternatively, you can freeze the dough before cooking it and cook the muffins on the day you want to eat them.

Defrosting and Reheating Directions:

1. Put muffins in the oven for 7 to 10 minutes or microwave them for a minute or two.

Buttermilk Pancakes

This is a basic recipe for buttermilk pancakes that can be tailored to suit your needs. Feel free to add blueberries, strawberries, peaches or even mashed bananas to the mix to add flavor.

Ingredients:

4 cups buttermilk

4 large eggs

1 stick butter, melted

½ cup sour cream

4 cups flour

3 tablespoons sugar

1 teaspoon salt

1 teaspoon baking soda

1 teaspoon baking powder

Vegetable oil, for cooking

Directions for Preparing and Freezing:

1. Add dry ingredients to a mixing bowl and whisk together.
2. Combine the wet ingredients (except for the vegetable oil) in a separate bowl and whisk together.

3. Make a well in the middle of the dry ingredients and pour the wet ingredients into it.
4. Stir the wet ingredients into the dry ingredients. You don't want to beat it until smooth. Leave the batter lumpy.
5. Let sit for 15 minutes.
6. Coat a skillet with a light coating of vegetable oil.
7. Pour ¼ cup of batter into skillet. This will make 1 small pancake. You can make them larger if you want.
8. Cook until one side is golden brown. Flip and cook the other side.
9. Let pancakes cool. Use Independent Quick Freezing to freeze the pancakes individually, and then transfer them into a freezer bag and freeze.

Defrosting and Reheating Directions:

1. Place in the toaster oven or in the toaster to defrost.
2. Heat until the pancakes start to get a little crispy on both sides.
3. Serve with your favorite topping.

Frozen Shrimp Egg Rolls

Whenever I go to a Chinese restaurant, I always order egg rolls. There are a couple of restaurants in my neighborhood that have egg rolls down to a science. When it comes to buying frozen egg rolls from the store, they can be really hit or miss. You're much better off making your own at home and freezing them.

You can freeze pretty much any egg roll you make and reheat it later. This is one food that does really well when frozen. They're a little bit harder to make than many of the other foods in this book, but you can make a bunch of them in one sitting and have them for weeks to come.

This recipe calls for shrimp, but you can sub in any meat you want. I've tried the same recipe with pork and with chicken and both were good.

Ingredients for Egg Roll Filling:

2 pounds shrimp

1 cup celery, diced

10 water chestnuts, thinly sliced

2 cups mushrooms, sliced

3 cups fresh bean sprouts

5 cups suey choy, shredded

2 onions, diced

2 garlic cloves, minced

3 tablespoons vegetable oil

20 egg roll wrappers

Ingredients for Egg Roll Sauce:

½ cup water

2 tablespoons cornstarch

4 teaspoons oyster sauce

2 teaspoons soy sauce

1 teaspoon sea salt

½ teaspoon pepper

Directions for Preparing and Freezing:

1. Add egg roll sauce ingredients to a glass bowl and whisk together. Set aside.
2. Add vegetable oil to a large skillet and cook shrimp over medium-high heat until they start to turn pink. Remove from the skillet and place on paper towel to drain. Chop shrimp into small pieces.
3. Lower the heat on the skillet to medium. Add the rest of the egg roll filling ingredients to the skillet and cook for 5 minutes, stirring occasionally.
4. Pour the sauce you made in step 1 into the skillet and stir until everything is coated with sauce. Cook for 5 more minutes or until done.
5. Remove from heat and add shrimp. Stir the shrimp into the mixture.
6. Lay out the egg roll wrapper and add a large spoonful of the mixture to the center of the egg roll.

Fold each of the corners in toward the center as shown in the image below:

7. Place each of the egg rolls onto a baking pan (or plate) with the seams facing down.
8. Place baking pan in the freezer for 45 minutes.
9. Transfer egg rolls to a freezer bag and store in freezer.

Defrosting and Reheating Directions:

1. Move egg rolls to refrigerator the night before you want to cook them so they can thaw out overnight.
2. Spray a baking sheet with cooking spray and place the egg rolls on them seam-side down.
3. Lightly brush the tops of the egg rolls with vegetable oil.

4. Preheat oven to 375°F and bake egg rolls for 15 to 17 minutes or until golden brown.

Note: Instead of freezing the uncooked egg rolls and then cooking them after thawing them out, you could cook them the day you roll them. This will allow you to pull them out of the freezer and microwave them when you want a quick snack. They won't taste quite as good as cooking them the day you want to eat them, but they're still pretty tasty.

Make-Ahead Pork Fried Rice

This rice is tasty and freezes well. You don't have to use pork if you don't want to. Chicken and shrimp work every bit as well with this recipe.

Ingredients:

10 cups cooked white rice

1 pound boiled chicken, cut into small pieces

1 cup frozen peas

5 eggs, beaten

2 carrots, diced

2 tablespoons rice vinegar

4 tablespoons soy sauce

2 tablespoons sesame oil

½ tablespoon sugar

½ teaspoon sea salt

A pinch of ground black pepper

¼ cup cooking oil

Directions for Preparing and Freezing:

1. Combine soy sauce, rice vinegar, sesame oil, sea salt, sugar and black pepper in a small bowl and stir together.
2. Add cooking oil to skillet or wok and place on medium-high heat.
3. Add chicken and stir-fry for 2 minutes.
4. Add eggs and cook until firm.

5. Add the rest of the ingredients and cook until vegetables are tender, stirring often.
6. Transfer into freezer bags and let cool in refrigerator for 45 minutes.
7. Move to freezer and freeze.

Defrosting and Reheating Directions:

1. Remove bag from freezer and place rice in glass bowl or dish.
2. Heat in microwave for 2 minutes.
3. Stir and heat for an additional minute or two.
4. Continue until rice is warmed all the way through.

Freezer Lasagna

If your husband is anything like my husband, you never know when he's going to show up with a friend in tow at dinner time. If I'm lucky, he'll call ahead and let me know he has someone with him so I'll have time to prepare something good for dinner.

Freezer lasagna is a good choice for those days he forgets to call. I try to always have at least a couple in the freezer, so I'm prepared to make a tasty meal at a moment's notice. They also make great gifts to give to people who are sick and have trouble cooking full meals or just had a baby.

The following recipe will make 1 lasagna.

Ingredients:

1 pound ground beef

2 onions, chopped

3 garlic cloves, minced

2 eggs

1 14.5oz can of diced tomatoes

2 cups tomato paste

1 cup tomato sauce

2 teaspoons Italian seasoning

2 cups ricotta cheese

2 cups shredded mozzarella cheese

10 cups water

10 lasagna noodles

2 teaspoons salt

1 teaspoon pepper

½ teaspoon basil

½ teaspoon oregano

2 tablespoons olive oil

½ cup Parmesan cheese, grated

¼ cup fresh parsley, chopped

Directions for Preparing and Freezing:

1. Add olive oil to a skillet and sauté onions and garlic for 5 minutes.
2. Add hamburger to skillet. Stir and cook until beef crumbles and starts to turn brown. Drain off excess grease and oil.
3. Add diced tomatoes, tomato paste, tomato sauce, Italian seasoning, salt, pepper and basil to the skillet and bring to a simmer for 25 minutes. Stir often.
4. Stir together Parmesan cheese, ricotta cheese, oregano and a pinch of salt and pepper. Add eggs and stir until incorporated.
5. Add 10 cups of water and 2 tablespoons of olive oil to a large pot and bring to a boil. Turn off heat and add lasagna. Let sit for 15 minutes.
6. Grease a 9" x 13" pan with butter and add half of the meat sauce to the pan. Make sure it's distributed evenly.
7. Lay 5 of the lasagna noodles over the meat sauce. Add half of the Parmesan-ricotta mixture and

spread it evenly, then cover with cover with 1 cup of shredded mozzarella.
8. Add the rest of the meat sauce and spread evenly.
9. Repeat step 7.
10. Wrap glass baking dish with plastic wrap. You want to cover it with at least 3 layers.
11. Place dish in refrigerator first and let it cool for ½ hour, then transfer the dish to the freezer.

Defrosting and Reheating Directions:

1. Whenever possible, take lasagna out the night before and let it thaw in the fridge. If not, you can pop it right in the oven, but you need to up the cooking time by 1 ½ times.
2. Preheat oven to 350°F and cook for 15 minutes. You'll know it's done when the cheese on top is starting to brown and the meat sauce and cheese is bubbling.

Honey Dijon Salmon

When you think of freezer meals, you typically don't think of meals that would fit right in on the menu at a fancy seafood restaurant. This recipe fits the bill, and it does so nicely. Cook it when you don't feel like eating something that feels like it's straight out of the freezer.

Ingredients:

4 salmon fillets

4 tablespoons honey

2 tablespoons Dijon mustard

2 tablespoons soy sauce

A pinch of black pepper

4 tablespoons olive oil

2 cloves minced garlic

Directions for Preparing and Freezing:

1. Create marinade by whisking honey, Dijon mustard, soy sauce, olive oil and garlic together in a bowl.
2. Add salmon filets and marinade to a large freezer bag and set in fridge for 1 hour.
3. Transfer to freezer and freeze.

Defrosting and Reheating Directions:

1. Thaw salmon overnight or cook frozen salmon. If you're cooking frozen salmon, it's going to take longer for it to cook.
2. Preheat oven to 350°F and cook salmon for 10 minutes (12 to 15 if frozen).

3. Sprinkle sliced green onions on top for garnish and serve.

Shredded Slow-Cooked Beef Sandwiches

This recipe can be handled in one of two ways. You can either cook the beef on the day you prepare your food or you can wait and cook it the day you eat your food. I've found cooking the beef on preparation day leaves it a little dry when you reheat it, but it's a lot faster than the second option. If you cook it on the day you plan on eating it, you have to remember to throw it in the slow cooker 8 to 10 hours before dinner time. I prefer this method, and I throw mine in the cooker before I leave for work and it's done when I get home.

Ingredients:

1 beef roast (3 to 5 pounds)

5 cups water

1 bay leaf

½ cup Worchester sauce

1 tablespoon dried rosemary

1 tablespoon dried basil

1 clove garlic, minced

Directions for Preparing and Freezing (If Cooking First):

1. Add all ingredients except for roast into a slow cooker and stir up.
2. Add roast.
3. Set on low heat and cook for 8 to 10 hours. Break roast up into pieces when it gets soft.

4. Take roast and juice and place it in a large freezer bag.
5. Set bag in fridge for 1 hour to cool, and then transfer to freezer.

Defrosting and Reheating Directions (If Cooking First):

1. Place frozen roast and juice in pot on medium heat and bring to a boil, stirring occasionally
2. Let boil for 5 minutes and remove from heat.
3. Remove roast from juice and place on a paper towel.
4. Place in hamburger buns or on rolls and serve with juice in a cup for dipping.

Directions for Preparing and Freezing (If Cooking Later):

1. Combine all ingredients except for roast in a large bowl and stir up.
2. Dump roast and sauce into a large freezer bag and place in fridge.
3. Let sit in fridge for a couple hours.
4. Transfer to freezer.

Defrosting and Reheating Directions (If Cooking First):

1. Remove bag from freezer and dump contents into slow cooker.
2. Set on low heat and cook for 8 to 10 hours or until roast is soft.
3. Break roast up into chunks and place on paper towel to drain.
4. Serve with juice from slow cooker.

Spaghetti and Meatball Casserole

I'm not a big fan of this one, but my kids absolutely love it. Nothing fancy here, just spaghetti and meatballs made into a casserole. This recipe is easy to whip up and you can make enough to feed an army. It tastes pretty much the same when it's fresh or when it's been frozen and thawed.

Ingredients:

1 pound of uncooked spaghetti noodles

½ pound of lean hamburger

2 cups of your favorite spaghetti sauce

1 onion, chopped

2 garlic cloves, minced

2 tablespoons olive oil

¼ cup milk

1 cup mozzarella cheese

1 cup parmesan cheese

Directions for Preparing and Freezing:

1. If you haven't done so already, boil spaghetti noodles until they're soft.
2. Add lean hamburger, olive oil, onion and garlic to a skillet and sauté until hamburger begins to brown.
3. Add spaghetti, spaghetti sauce and milk and bring to a simmer. Let simmer for 5 minutes.
4. Pour into a 9" x 13" casserole dish.
5. Sprinkle mozzarella and parmesan cheese on top, to taste.

6. Place casserole dish in fridge for 30 minutes to let cool.
7. Cover with plastic wrap (at least 3 layers) and place in freezer.

Defrosting and Reheating Directions:

1. Top frozen casserole with aluminum foil.
2. Preheat oven to 375°F and bake for 30 minutes.
3. Remove foil and bake for another 5 to 10 minutes, or until cheese starts to brown.

Freezer Cheesy Garlic Bread

Make your garlic bread ahead of time and freeze it and you'll save a lot of time in the kitchen. This garlic bread is the perfect addition to any Italian meal.

Ingredients:

1 loaf French bread

10 tablespoons butter

3 cloves garlic, minced

3 tablespoons Italian seasoning

½ cup grated mozzarella cheese

½ cup grated parmesan cheese

Directions for Preparing and Freezing:

1. Slice loaf of bread in half lengthwise.
2. Combine all ingredients in a small glass bowl and stir until incorporated.
3. Spread the garlic butter evenly onto each half of the loaf of bread.
4. Mix the parmesan and mozzarella cheeses and sprinkle on top of each half loaf.
5. Close the loaf, wrap it in plastic wrap and freeze.

Defrosting and Heating Directions:

1. Preheat oven to 375°F.
2. Place half a loaf on a baking sheet with the open side facing up.
3. Bake for 15 to 20 minutes or until the cheese on top starts to brown.

Mini Meatloaf Bites

These little mini meatloaves are the perfect size for a snack or you can serve a couple of them with a side or two for dinner. I hadn't seen or heard of these until a friend served them at a Super Bowl party a few years back. I fell in love and started making them with my meatloaf recipe.

Don't let the long ingredient list fool you. Mini meatloaf bites are easy to make.

Ingredients for Preparing:

3 pounds lean ground beef or turkey

1 ½ cups breadcrumbs

½ cup ketchup

2 green peppers, diced

1 medium onion, diced

½ cup bacon, broken into pieces

½ cup diced tomatoes

1 clove of garlic, minced

½ teaspoon oregano

½ teaspoon basil

½ teaspoon ground black pepper

½ cup fresh parsley, chopped

3 eggs

A pinch of salt

A pinch of pepper

Directions for Preparing and Freezing:

1. Mix all of the ingredients except for the bacon and barbecue sauce in a large mixing bowl.
2. Spray a muffin tin with a light coating of cooking spray.
3. Fill each space in the muffin tin ¾ full with meatloaf mixture.
4. Sprinkle bacon on top and press into meatloaf.
5. Place muffin tin in freezer and let freeze.
6. Remove frozen meatloaf bites from the muffin tin and place in a large freezer bag.

Ingredients for Cooking:

½ cup barbecue sauce

1 cup shredded cheddar cheese

Defrosting and Cooking Directions:

1. Preheat oven to 400°F.
2. Take meatloaf bites out of the bag and place each one in its own space in a muffin tin.
3. Bake for 20 minutes.
4. Remove from oven and brush tops with barbecue sauce. I prefer Sweet Baby Ray's, but you can use whatever sauce you want.
5. Sprinkle cheese on top and bake until cheese starts to bubble.
6. Let cool for 5 minutes and serve warm.

Baked Whole Wheat Penne Casserole with Sausage

This one's a comfort food that's great for stormy winter days. It's rich and tasty and a small serving fills you up. The recipe calls for whole wheat pasta, but you can use whatever kind of pasta you like. I substitute in macaroni when I feel like changing things up a bit.

Ingredients:

16 ounces of your favorite sausage

16 ounces of whole wheat penne pasta

16 ounces ricotta cheese

2 cups fresh mozzarella cheese, shredded

¼ cup parmesan cheese

2 cups tomato puree

1 garlic clove, minced

3 cups water

½ teaspoon ground fennel

1 bay leaf

1 teaspoon plus a pinch of salt

Pinch of pepper

Directions for Preparing and Freezing:

1. Add olive oil to saucepan. Break up sausage and cook it over medium heat. Cook until the sausage is browned.

2. Add garlic, tomato puree, 1 cup water, a pinch of salt and pepper, fennel and bay leaf. Let simmer for 30 minutes, or until it starts to thicken.
3. In a separate pot, add 2 cups water and bring to a boil. Add 1 teaspoon of salt to the water and stir in. Add pasta and let boil until soft. Once soft, drain the water off the pasta.
4. Combine meat sauce and pasta in the pot. Save approximately 1 cup of meat sauce. Stir sauce and pasta until it's evenly distributed.
5. Pour pasta into 9" x 13" glass baking dish and distribute evenly. Pour the remaining meat sauce on top.
6. Distribute cheeses over the top and fold into mixture. You want to fold it in so there are pockets of cheese spread throughout the casserole.
7. The dish is complete and ready to be frozen. Cover with at least 3 layers of plastic wrap and put it in the freezer.

Ingredients for Defrosting and Reheating:

½ cup mozzarella cheese, shredded

Defrosting and Reheating Directions:

1. Sprinkle mozzarella cheese on top.
2. Cover frozen casserole with aluminum foil.
3. Preheat oven to 375°F and bake for 55 minutes.
4. Remove foil and bake for another 5 to 10 minutes, or until cheese starts to brown.

Grilled Chicken Skewers

I love barbecued chicken skewers. The only problem is where I live, it's too cold to go outside and barbecue for a good portion of the year. Instead of only enjoying barbecued chicken skewers for a few months every year, I make extra skewers every time I barbecue and toss them in the freezer. That way, I can enjoy grilled chicken skewers year-round.

Ingredients:

2 pounds boneless, skinless chicken, cut into 1-inch cubes

1 cup honey

2 tablespoons lime juice

2 tablespoons ground cinnamon

½ tablespoon cayenne pepper

¼ cup sesame seeds

½ teaspoon turmeric

½ teaspoon paprika

Sea salt, to taste

Wooden skewers

Directions for Preparing and Freezing:

1. Combine all ingredients in a mixing bowl and stir until blended.
2. Place chicken and mixture into a freezer bag and let marinate in the fridge overnight.
3. Place wooden skewers in a bowl of water and let them soak for 10 minutes.

4. Place chicken on skewers and grill until the chicken is cooked all the way through.
5. Let skewers cool and place them in a plastic freezer bag.
6. Freeze.

Defrosting and Reheating Directions:

1. Remove skewers from freezer the night before you want to serve them and place them in the fridge to thaw.
2. Preheat oven to 350°F and cook for 15 minutes or until heated all the way through.
3. Serve hot.

Other Titles by This Author

The Quinoa Cookbook: Healthy and Delicious Quinoa Recipes

http://www.amazon.com/The-Quinoa-Cookbook-Delicious-ebook/dp/B00B2T2420

Quinoa is said to be one of the most complete and healthy foods known to man. Learn how to clean and cook quinoa and add this tasty superfood to your diet today. Buy the *The Quinoa Cookbook* now and find out what you've been missing!

Printed in Great Britain
by Amazon